Mother, wherever I go...
whatever I do...
I will always carry your
love in my heart.

Titles by Marci
Published by
Blue Mountain Arts®

Angels Are Everywhere!
Angels Bring a Message
of Hope Whenever It Is Needed

Friends Are Forever
A Gift of Inspirational Thoughts
to Thank You for Being
My Friend

10 Simple Things to Remember
An Inspiring Guide to
Understanding Life

To My Daughter
Love and Encouragement
to Carry with You on Your
Journey Through Life

To My Granddaughter
A Gift of Love and Wisdom
to Always Carry
in Your Heart

To My Mother
I Will Always Carry
Your Love in My Heart

To My Sister
A Gift of Love and Inspiration
to Thank You
for Being My Sister

To My Son
Love and Encouragement
to Carry with You on Your
Journey Through Life

You Are My "Once in a Lifetime"
I Will Always Love You

To My Mother

I Will Always Carry Your Love in My Heart

Marci

Blue Mountain Press™

Boulder, Colorado

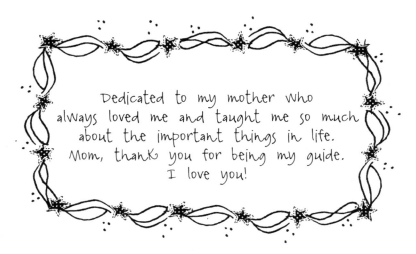

Dedicated to my mother who
always loved me and taught me so much
about the important things in life.
Mom, thanks you for being my guide.
I love you!

Library of Congress Control Number: 2012940480
ISBN: 978-1-59842-687-8

Children of the Inner Light is a registered trademark. Used under license.
Certain trademarks are used under license.

Printed in China.
Fifth Printing: 2015

♻ This book is printed on recycled paper.

This book is printed on paper that has been specially produced to be acid free (neutral pH) and contains no groundwood or unbleached pulp. It conforms with the requirements of the American National Standards Institute, Inc., so as to ensure that this book will last and be enjoyed by future generations.

Blue Mountain Arts, Inc.
P.O. Box 4549, Boulder, Colorado 80306

Contents

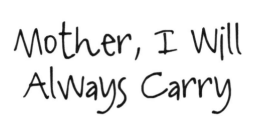

Mother, I Will
Always Carry

Your Love
in My Heart

Wherever I go… whatever I do… I will always carry your love in my heart. Your love becomes hope and makes life's challenges bearable. Your love becomes faith and inspires me to do my best. Your love stays in my heart each and every hour of the day and reminds me that I am not alone. I am so glad that I have you in my life.

I Know I Don't
Tell You This Enough...

but Please Remember
How Much I Love You

Even if I do not say so, I believe you are the best mom anyone could ever have. Thank you for believing in me... for your constant love and prayers... and for all the little things you do each day just because you love me. I am so fortunate you are my mother.

Some of us are so blessed to have a special person whom we cannot imagine life without... a person who is ever present in spirit... whose care and concern are known and felt even from a distance... and whose love and friendship are always given as gifts. I am the one so blessed... and you are the reason why!

You've Made
Such a Difference

in My Life

Mother, I think of you so often and realize just how special you are. You have made such a difference in my life. For the many kind words you have spoken, for the thoughtful things you have done, for the way you are always there sharing the special person you are... thank you!

Remember when you sent me off to my first day of school? You had every little detail just right so my beginning would be perfect.

Remember all my birthdays you celebrated to remind me how much I was loved? And how you always found a special card?

Remember the hugs of encouragement and the tears you dried along the way?

Remember the worries you had as I was finding my way in the world? And how you "let me go" even though it was hard?

I remember all those things, and as I look back, I feel so loved. Thank you for being there and for being my mother!

Time Has Shown Me

the Lasting Treasure
of Your Love

Time has brought me a greater understanding of life and a growing appreciation of all you have been to me. As life's plan unfolds and I am gifted with the experience of living, I see you in a new light. I truly know the love you have given and felt over the years, and I am filled with gratitude.

You've Given Me
Everything I Need
in Life...

and More!

On the day I was born, I was given a beautiful gift... the gift of having you as my mother. I want you to always remember how thankful I am for this blessing and how much I treasure the priceless things you have given so freely. There is the faith you've shown in me that has allowed me to believe in myself... there is the love you've given me that has taught me to love with all my heart... and there are the values you demonstrated that have given me a foundation for living. These are the gifts that will be with me always.

You taught me so many important things... to be on time, to be committed, to work hard, to give my best, to love completely, to sacrifice, and, no matter what, to trust in God. It was the example you set as you quietly and consistently lived your beliefs that had an impact on me. These lessons have made the difference between my being successful and just getting through.

You showed me that love is found in commitment. You demonstrated that sacrifice does make one stronger. You gave so much of yourself to your family that you taught me the beautiful reward found in giving. You taught me that everything happens for a reason, even if we never understand it. And you showed me that love never ends, which is the most important lesson of all! You are my mother, my mentor, my guide.

From you, I Learned...

the Five Keys to Happiness

1. That happiness is a choice... I can make the decision to "be happy" each day.

2. That happiness is contagious... When I make someone smile, the good feelings come right back to me.

3. To be grateful for the little things in life that are free... to make a list and add to it each morning.

4. To believe that ultimately everything happens for a reason. Acceptance leads the way to happiness.

5. To give away some courage every day because encouraging another to "keep going," "hang in there," or "believe in your dreams" is an unending source of happiness.

Sometimes we get so caught up in our own busy lives that we forget to connect with the people who are so important to us. Time flies by, and we put off saying "I love you" until tomorrow. I hope you always Know how I feel... and how much your hugs, encouragement, and prayers will always mean to me. I love you!

The Angel in
My Life Is...

you!

Angels are at work in our lives every day... Watching over us, prompting us to be compassionate, reminding us to pray, and sometimes working through others to bring an unexpected kindness that makes us stop and realize just how wonderful and giving the human spirit is! I feel so blessed to be the recipient of your kindness and so grateful too. The angel in my life is... you!

Angels Are Everywhere

You held me as a baby and let me come into your heart. You nurtured me through childhood and taught me the values that would carry me through life. At times, you let me learn from my own mistakes, but you were always there to dry my tears and share my joys.

You have watched me take my journey and inspired me along the way. You have shared my happiness in everything I do... and you do it all just because you are my mother! I am so glad to have been blessed with a mother like you.

Mothers Have So Much

Love to Share

Everything mothers are a part of turns into something great and wonderful. They are always there to answer the call, whether it's a call to love... a call to sacrifice... a call to give and receive... or a call to feel joy and sorrow to the depths of their being. Theirs is the love that is always with you. It is one of the treasures in life that lasts forever.

Mother,
You Have Shown Me

the True Meaning
of Family

Families are special creations made up of people who love each other and are tied together with threads of common experience, memories, and values. You are such a special part of our family and a gift to me every day.

Because of you...

I Always Have Someone
I Can Turn To

Having a mother like you means
I always have a hand to hold...
an ear to listen...
a heart to understand...
a hug to comfort me...
some words of wisdom...
and a bright light
to guide my way!

Your Positive Spirit

Hope

Is Contagious

When my path seems to be filled with roadblocks and I wonder why life is so difficult, you remind me that hope is a gift we can give to ourselves... When we choose this attitude and tap into our inner reserves, we are rewarded with the knowledge of what we have learned in life. The decision to look forward, stay positive, and remain hopeful is a key that unlocks the door to possibilities, and you show me every day the power of hope.

Some people have a special light around them from the day they are born... It shines brightly and makes them stand out in a crowd. You are one of those people! Your heart is always open, ready to share or just listen to those in need. Your arms are always ready with a hug and a reminder that God has a plan. Thank you for the inspiration you are and for the bright light that shines as you. You are a shining star!

A Mother Is...

A mother is a guiding force through the journey of life.

A mother is the one with the heart that always understands.

A mother is always there through good times and bad.

A mother is a gift provided
by a greater plan.

A mother is a teacher, a
mentor, a friend.

A mother is the one who
will always love you.

Mother...

I Appreciate You
More and More
Each Day

I am so happy to have you in my life. You are the one I look to when I need guidance. You are the one I hold on to when I need support. You are the one I go to when I need help. You put so much love into everything you do, and I appreciate you more and more every day. Thank you for being you!

I Am Proud to Call You...

My Mother

You are the mother that everyone wants... You are loving and encouraging... You are there with whatever is needed... And you love me no matter what.

Through the years I have told you how much I love you, but have I told you how much I appreciate you and how proud I am to say that you are my mother?

You Are More Than
Just a Special Mother...

You Are a Special Person

You have a way of always brightening my day... and it's with little things that mean so much. There is a phone call at just the right time, a hug when it is needed, or a comforting word of encouragement. You are a quiet, steady, burning light that inspires me to be my best.

Whenever I Need You...

You're Always There

Some days I just need a hand to hold... Some days I just need a hug... Some days I just need a word of encouragement... Some days I just need someone to be there for a laugh and a memory... On my "some days" there is you!

You See the Best in Me

...and Help Me to See It Too

You see the "real me" shining through no matter what is happening. You love me through the hard times and beam with joy through the best times. You look at me with pride for even my smallest accomplishments. As only a mother can, you show me how much you care.

You Believe in Me

...No Matter What

You are the one who believes in me no matter what... who celebrates my strengths and doesn't seem to notice my weaknesses... who is there for me through thick and thin, always inspiring me to do my best. I can count on you to be the one who says, "You can do it"... "Hang in there"... and "Everything's going to be okay." I just want you to know how very much this means to me.

You must have had so many dreams for me when I was born, but you let me have my own dreams and supported me through them too.

You watched me grow and change each year, always reminding me to be true to myself in all of life's challenges.

You gave me opportunities that helped me discover who I am and gave me the tools I would need to succeed.

You reminded me so often that I was truly loved, and these times have given me so many precious little moments to save.

You let me go when I am sure you wanted to hold on, and that gave me confidence to find my place in the world.

In so many ways, you have shown me unconditional love.

It Is Hard
to Find the Words
to Let You Know

How Much You Mean
to Me

I am so thankful for all you have given over the years but mostly for the special person you are. It is not just the love and concern you have shown... the help given whenever it was needed... or the model you have been. It is all those things wrapped into one and given with love and a sense of constancy.

If I Searched the World...

I Could Never Find a Better Mother

You are a perfect example of love and caring, compassion and concern. Just talking to you can make me feel better, and being with you reminds me of the most important things in life. Knowing that I have a mother like you is a gift of family and friendship wrapped up in love!

When I was young, I did not understand all that a mother gives through the years... but as I have grown, I have realized just how much your patience and encouragement have fostered my growth, and I have come to understand just how special you are.

Your love has been never-ending... the important things you taught me are life enriching... and the model you gave me for "how to live" shines a light that guides me through life. I am grateful to you for these gifts and for being my mother!

For All the Little Things You Do...

Please Know...

Sometimes I forget to say
"thanks" for all the little things
you do... but I want you to
know that even when I do
not say so, I am so thankful for
your thoughtfulness, your caring,
your willingness to please. your
efforts never go unnoticed...

For all the meals you planned... for the endless cleaning up... for the homework you sat through... for the illnesses you tended... for the holidays you made special... for the faith you shared with me... for the sense of family you provided...

I thank you from the
bottom of my heart.

Love Is the Gift

You Give Me
Each Day

Thank you for
the life you gave me,
the tears you dried,
the encouragement given,
the lessons taught,
the joys shared,
the hard times hugged away,
and especially just for
being my mother!

There Is Nothing Greater Than...

A MOTHER'S LOVE
SHINES
EVERY DAY!

A Mother's Love

A mother's love is everlasting.

A mother's love is a guiding light.

A mother's love is a gift that we understand through time.

A mother's love is a blessing that will be always in our hearts.

Mother, I Hold in My Heart...

So Many Wishes for You

I wish you happiness as you begin
each day... special love to warm
your heart... and tender memories
to store away.

I wish that you know how much
I appreciate the mother you are
to me and remember that I love
you this day and every day...

I wish you peace... peace in
knowing who you are... peace in
knowing what you believe in...
and peace in the understanding
of what is important in life.

I wish you joy... joy as you awaken each day with gratitude in your heart for new beginnings... joy when you surrender to the beauty of a flower or a baby's smile... and joy, a hundred times returned, for each time you've brought happiness to another's heart.

The Older I Get, the More I Realize...

All That You've Given to Me

When I was young, I thought the years didn't pass quickly enough, and I couldn't wait to be one year older. Then, in what seems like "suddenly," I was older! When I look back now and wonder where the time has gone, I realize the road behind me is full of the gifts that make us rich: hard-earned wisdom... an appreciation for family... trials that made me stronger... hope given to others... prayers answered... love given and received. These are all things that you've given to me.

Many moments and days of love.

Opening your heart to me.

Time... a precious gift.

Home... a place to be loved.

Everlasting memories.

Remembering to say, "I love you."

Many moments and days of love.

Opening your heart to me.

Time... a precious gift.

Home... a place to be loved.

Everlasting memories.

I Asked Your
Guardian Angel

to Watch Over You

I prayed for you today and asked your guardian angel to stay by your side... to bring you inspiration when life gets you down... to fill your heart with determination when life puts obstacles in your path... and to shower you with grace to nurture your spiritual growth as you travel your path through life...

I lit a candle for you today in my heart... a flame of love and prayer that burns with the hope that God's grace finds its way to you every day... protects you from worry... and fills your heart with unshakable faith in difficult times.

I asked that you feel the love of God like a gentle breeze when you need encouragement... and that hope be the burning light that always guides your way.

May You
Be Filled with...

Lasting Happiness

May your days be filled
with all the things that
will bring you lasting
happiness. May faith guide
your path toward your
dreams... may hope be a
constant light in your
life... and may love warm
your heart every day.

Mother...

Our Bond Is
Everlasting

I have come to understand and accept that our lives have been brought together for a reason, and for that I am grateful. Your love is what I needed to grow to my fullest potential. I am grateful for the person you are and for your love and caring over the years. You have seen my best and my worst and have loved me. The bond we have found is everlasting.

Give Yourself
a Hug Today

from Me!

I want you to always know and remember what you mean to me. The joys we have shared and the memories we have made through our lives are a gift beyond measure. Thank you for your love. Today, consider yourself hugged!

Only My Heart Can Truly Express

Just How Much You Mean to Me

You are the light that shines in my life when I need inspiration... you are the arms that hug me when I need consoling... you are the person I rely on to listen when I just need to be heard. You are the one who says the things I most need to hear... I want you to know how blessed I feel each and every day to have a mother like you.

There have never been words
more powerful than
"I love you"...
or more meaningful than
"Thank you"...
So I'm saying these things
to you now:
"I love you more
than words can say,
and I am so thankful
you are a part of my life."

About Marci

Marci began her career by hand painting floral designs on clothing. No one was more surprised than she was when one day, in a single burst of inspiration and a completely new and different art style, her delightful characters sprang from her pen! "Their wild and crazy hair is a sign of strength," she thought, "and their crooked little smiles are endearing." She quickly identified the charming characters as Mother, Daughter, Sister, Father, Son, Friend, and so on until all the people and places in life were filled. Then, with her own loved ones in mind, she wrote a true and special sentiment to each one. This would be the beginning of a wonderful success story, which today still finds Marci writing each and every one of her verses in this same personal way.

Marci is a self-taught artist who has always enjoyed writing and art. She is thrilled to see how her delightful characters and universal messages of love have touched the hearts and lives of people everywhere. Her distinctive designs can also be found on Blue Mountain Arts greeting cards, calendars, bookmarks, and other gift items.

To learn more about Marci, look for Children of the Inner Light on Facebook or visit her website: WWW.MARCIonline.com.